Written by
HEATHER ALEXANDER

Illustrated by
SAM KALDA

HAUNTED U.S.A.

WIDE EYED EDITIONS

CONTENTS

Prepare for a Scare!	4	Iowa	34
Alabama	6	Kansas	36
Alaska	8	Kentucky	38
Arizona	10	Louisiana	40
Arkansas	12	Maine	42
California	14	Maryland	44
Colorado	16	Massachusetts	46
Connecticut	18	Michigan	48
Delaware	20	Minnesota	50
Florida	22	Mississippi	52
Georgia	24	Missouri	54
Hawaii	26	Montana	56
Idaho	28	Nebraska	58
Illinois	30	Nevada	60
Indiana	32	New Hampshire	62

New Jersey	64	Vermont	94
New Mexico	66	Virginia	96
New York	68	Washington	98
North Carolina	70	West Virginia	100
North Dakota	72	Wisconsin	102
Ohio	74	Wyoming	104
Oklahoma	76	Washington, D.C.	106
Oregon	78	A Ghost Hunter's Guide	108
Pennsylvania	80	Spooky Glossary	110
Rhode Island	82		
South Carolina	84		
South Dakota	86		
Tennessee	88		
Texas	90		
Utah	92		

PREPARE FOR A SCARE!

ARE YOU BRAVE ENOUGH TO JOURNEY THROUGH THE HAUNTED UNITED STATES?

Join us, if you dare, as we travel around the nation to delight in the spookiest legends, visit the eeriest places, meet the creepiest creatures, and encounter ghosts of all shapes and sizes. There are haunted houses (of course!), haunted zoos, haunted amusement parks, haunted ships, and even a haunted library. Strange creatures lurk in forests and swim in deep lakes and—*think fast!*—may be sneaking up on you right now. Are you scared yet? We sure are! And there's more—you'll meet ghosts you can see through, ghosts that play music, ghosts that gallop, ghosts that tap dance, and ghosts that will eat your chocolate!

Now for the big question: are ghosts real? There's no correct answer. Some people claim to have seen, heard, or interacted with them. Others say it's not possible. Many of us are unsure, since what happens after death is still very much a mystery. One thing we do know is everyone (well, almost everyone) loves a good scary story. And that's what these are—spook-tacular tales and legends. Whether you're at home, on a family road trip, at a sleepover, or around a campfire, get ready to get goosebumps with a spine-tingling tale from each of the fifty states. Oh, yes—an important warning: you're going to want to read this book with the lights on!

ALABAMA
GHOSTS JUST WANNA HAVE FUN

When the sun shines bright, the sound of children's laughter rings out in a playground in Huntsville. Kids scramble across the jungle gym and chase one another in the shade of the looming trees. They pump their legs and lean back on the swings, hoping to touch the sky. When night falls, these children are at home, tucked snuggly into bed. So that should mean this playground is silent and empty, right? Wrong! Children are still at play, swinging and laughing by the light of the moon. But you won't be able to see them or join in the fun. These kids are ghosts.

The small playground is next to Maple Hill Cemetery, tucked away in a low area surrounded by trees and limestone boulders. Maple Hill was built in 1822, making it the oldest cemetery in the state. It's also the largest. Hundreds of thousands of people are buried here. Many were victims of the Spanish flu. (Despite its name, researchers believe the Spanish flu most likely started in the United States.) In 1918, this virus infected millions around the world. It was much worse than the regular flu, or influenza. Doctors were baffled by the disease. They didn't have medicine to treat it or know how to stop it from spreading. In school yards, kids jumped rope to the new chant:

Others have witnessed the swings moving on their own.

"I had a little bird
And its name was Enza,
I opened the window
And in-flew-Enza!"

Many of the children in Huntsville who didn't survive the Spanish flu are said to have been buried in grave sites near the playground—and legend has it their spirits come out to play after dark! Passersby have reported seeing ghostly kids on the equipment. Others have witnessed the swings moving on their own. There have been reports of laughter in the darkness and children happily calling out to one another. And that's not all! When some nighttime photographs of the playground were developed, orbs of ghostly light appeared in the pictures. Could these have been the cemetery kids?

ALASKA
OTTERLY TERRIFYING

Have you ever seen pictures of playful otters frolicking in an ocean or river? These tiny, furry, marine mammals couldn't be more adorable if they tried. But don't be fooled by all the cuteness—something sinister is afloat!

For centuries, the Tlingit people of southeastern Alaska have told stories of the Kushtaka (or Kóoshdaa káa), a shape-shifting creature that can take the form of a large otter, a human, or a half-otter, half-man creature. As one legend goes, a person wandering through the snowy Alaskan woods or along the icy shore will first hear a distinctive three-note whistle. Low, high, then low again. They will probably shrug it off, not realizing it's the warning call of the Kushtaka. A little while later, they'll meet a friendly traveler or, perhaps, spot an adorable otter swimming nearby. How lovely to have some company, they'll think. They'll chat with the traveler or play with the otter. Suddenly, the anguished cry of a baby or the scream of a woman will ring out. Quick—someone is in danger!

The person will rush into the wilderness to rescue them but won't be able to find anyone. The cries were a trick. And at that moment, the traveler or the cute otter will shape-shift into the huge, hairy Kushtaka! With a growl and a roar, the creature will turn the shocked person into a Kushtaka too, trapping their soul in an otter's body for all eternity.

They will probably shrug it off, not realizing it's the warning call of the Kushtaka.

Too bad our victim didn't have a dog. It's believed Kushtakas are terrified of dogs, and a dog's bark can force them to reveal their true selves. It's also said a Kushtaka can be driven away with copper, fire, and urine. So remember: always travel with a dog and be ready to pee!

Other versions of the Tlingit legend tell of a friendly Kushtaka, who appears to lost travelers to help them find their way out of the wilderness. It seems you never know what kind of beast you may meet in rugged, remote Alaska.

ARIZONA
THE BONEYARD

A pilot in an Army Air Corps-issued leather flight jacket walked slowly through the rows of old airplanes. He squinted in the mid-day sun at the names and numbers painted on their sides, searching desperately for his beloved fighter plane. He'd once guided her through thick clouds, dodging enemy fire in terrifying air-to-air combat missions. Together, they had rolled up and out in amazing bursts of speed. So where had they put her now? The World War II ace retraced his path again and again. His footsteps were eerily soundless, as if his boots failed to make contact with the ground. The pilot was a phantom.

The airman doomed to forever search for his plane is one of several ghosts said to haunt the United States' largest boneyard. What's a boneyard? It's a graveyard for airplanes. The 309th Aerospace Maintenance and Regeneration Group boneyard at Davis-Monthan Air Force Base in Tucson is the final resting place for about four thousand of the nation's military aircraft. Retired and out-of-service flying machines, including World War II bombers, are stored here. Some are waiting to be called back into service, and some will be broken down and used for spare parts. It's the largest military boneyard in the world.

It seems airplane cemeteries may also be haunted.

Here, row upon row of grounded warbirds stand at attention in the hot desert. The blazing sun reflects off their silent, unmoving metal bodies. The storage site was chosen because Arizona's dry air, low humidity, and little rainfall help keep the aircraft from getting rusty. The hard, dry soil lets the planes be moved without sinking into the ground and without needing to create pavement. But just like with human cemeteries, it seems airplane cemeteries may also be haunted. Some guests on the base claimed to have spotted the spirits of aviators near the World War II planes. Then they disappear, sometimes walking right through fences! Security guards have reported flashlights not working and the headlights of their patrol vehicles blinking or going dark. Perhaps the ghosts who once ruled the sky aren't happy to be permanently grounded.

ARKANSAS
THE GURDON LIGHT

Are you brave enough to search for the mysterious Gurdon Light? A glowing orb of blue-white, or sometimes yellow-orange, light is said to float eerily above a deserted stretch of railroad tracks outside Gurdon, a small town in southwest Arkansas. What is the light? Where does it come from? No one has been able to explain it, but here's one of the more popular legends.

A long time ago, a railroad worker was fixing the track late at night. Thick, swampy forest surrounded him on either side. He felt the familiar rumble of an approaching train vibrate the steel track. He calculated that he still had plenty of time to finish the repair. But when he was finally done, he stumbled and accidentally fell onto the track. Before he could scramble out of the way, the headlights of the oncoming locomotive blinded him and—bam! The speeding train hit him so hard his head flew off his body. Ever since then, his ghost has wandered these railroad tracks, swinging a lantern to and fro in search of his missing head. It seems he will not rest until it is found.

Many believe the strange, round, bobbing light is the lantern of the headless ghost but there are other, less spooky, theories. The reflection of car headlights was once offered as a non-ghostly explanation, but the railroad tracks are too far away from Interstate 30 for that theory to hold up. Also, stories about the light were told back in the 1930s, decades before the highway was built. In fact, some people say the light dates back centuries, way before the tale of the unfortunate railroad worker even. If so, one theory is that swamp gas may create the light. Another has to do with all the underground quartz crystal in the area. The shifting earth is known to make electricity rise off the quartz and maybe this causes the glow. Both scientific theories are valid, but neither has been fully proven. And no photographer has been able to snap a good picture of the floating light. What do you think? Are you Team Science or Team Headless Ghost?

No photographer has been able to snap a good picture of the floating light.

CALIFORNIA
HOME IS WHERE THE HORROR IS

The Winchester Mystery House in San Jose has been called one of the greatest haunted houses ever built. What does it take to win First-in-Fright? Major tragedy, an overwhelming fear and fascination with ghosts, and lots of folklore.

The story starts with the marriage of Sarah Pardee to William Winchester in 1862. His family was super wealthy, but life was not kind to Sarah. Their baby died of an illness and, soon after, William died of tuberculosis. Sarah blamed angry spirits and hired mediums to communicate with her dead husband. In one séance, his ghost allegedly said that the only way to keep the angry spirits away was to move west and build an enormous new home. If she never stopped building it, nothing bad would happen.

> *If she never stopped building it, nothing bad would happen.*

So Sarah bought a small farmhouse near San Jose and started to build. And build. And build. Money wasn't an issue, as William had left her more than twenty million dollars. With most houses, carpenters follow plans drawn by an architect. Not Sarah's. From 1886 to 1922, she designed the house herself, haphazardly adding rooms in various sizes. Her only plan: keep the construction going—forever.

The house grew massive with 160 rooms, six kitchens, 10,000 windows, and 2,000 doors! Servants needed a map to find their way through the maze-like hallways. Staircases and chimneys led nowhere. Cabinets hid elaborate secret passageways. One door opened into a solid wall and another to an eight-foot drop. Sarah believed the number thirteen could keep evil spirits away, so she built thirteen bathrooms. Each chandelier had thirteen lights, the dining table had thirteen chairs, and the rooms had thirteen windows. Legend has it that every night Sarah slept in a different bedroom, so the ghosts couldn't find her.

After Sarah died, the house became a tourist attraction, and the spirits may have stayed on. Tour guides have reported Sarah's ghost in the bedroom where she died, and visitors have felt gentle tugs on their shirts or skirts. Some employees said they've seen a mustached man in old-fashioned work clothes pushing a wheelbarrow in the basement or repairing the fireplace in the ballroom. The odor of simmering soup has been detected in non-working kitchens, and some visitors claim to have heard the bell in the bell tower chime thirteen times in a row!

Is this haunted house story true or a sensational myth made up to excite tourists? You can investigate for yourself—the spooky house is eager to welcome you inside!

COLORADO
THE DOCTOR WILL SEE YOU NOW

The children leaned in to examine the old photographs of Black cowboys, ranchers, miners, homesteaders, and tradespeople. They'd come to the Black American West Museum & Heritage Center in Denver to learn about the pioneers who traveled into the Rocky Mountains long ago to develop the West. This school group was much like others that visited the museum. When they moved onto the next exhibit, one distracted kid always lagged behind. That's when a new tour guide would materialize. She was always the same woman, who reached out and gently held the hand of the turned-around kid, guiding them back to the group. Along the way, she might point out a few unnoticed, interesting details. And then she disappeared. But when the kid told the others, no one else would have seen or heard her.

She definitely wasn't an official museum employee. In fact, she may not have even been alive! The ghostly guide may be the spirit of Dr. Justina Ford. In 1902, Dr. Ford became the first Black woman in Colorado to receive her medical license. But back then, because of racism and sexism, hospitals in Denver wouldn't let her practice medicine. She'd dreamed of being a doctor since she was a child, had worked hard to achieve it, and refused to let discrimination stop her. Ford and her husband bought a two-story brick house in the Five Points area of Denver. Here, she treated patients turned away from hospitals because of racism or because they couldn't pay or couldn't speak English. She loved caring for kids and delivered more than seven thousand babies in her lifetime! In 1950, two years before she died at age 81, the Colorado Medical Society finally officially recognized her, making her the first Black female doctor in Colorado.

This doctor is forever on call.

In 1984 Dr. Ford's home became the Black American West Museum & Heritage Center. Her office and waiting room became part of the exhibits, so her ghost may still be hanging around, caring for kids. Former employees have told of hearing phantom footsteps upstairs and the mysterious opening and closing of doors. It seems this doctor is forever on call!

CONNECTICUT
BEWARE, THE BLACK DOG

If you ever go hiking in the Hanging Hills, volcanic rocky ridges in south central Connecticut, be very careful. A mysterious black dog is said to roam the wooded trails. This ghostly canine will not chase or bite you, but the mere sight of it can be deadly! As the legend goes, seeing this dog once will bring you joy. If you see it twice, you'll be overwhelmed with sadness. And if you're unlucky enough to see it three times, you will die.

The story of the cursed black dog of Hanging Hills first appeared in the 1898 edition of *Connecticut Quarterly* magazine in a piece written by William H. C. Pynchon. Some say it's pure fiction, but others believe the author based it on a real encounter. Here's the tale that was told:

The dog never barked or left prints in the dirt or snow.

In 1891, a geologist came to this part of Connecticut to study the land. As he gathered rocks, a black dog wandered over. The small, scruffy dog never made a sound, just silently followed him throughout the day. But when the geologist got ready to leave, the dog vanished.

Three years later, the same geologist returned to Hanging Hills during the winter to continue his research. He met up with a friend and, as they hiked through the deep snow, he told him about the strange dog. The friend too had seen this same black dog on his previous trips to the park. Not once, but twice! The dog never barked or left prints in the dirt or snow. How odd, they agreed, as they climbed the icy cliffs. Later that day, the black dog appeared on a rock above.

In the bitter cold, the dog stared down at them. Then it bounded away. At that moment, the fragment of rock the geologist's friend stood on suddenly broke free, sending him plummeting to his death. Scared and distraught, the geologist hurried away before the dog showed up again. But another three years later, he was in the area again, for research he needed to complete. Sadly, he never did. His body was discovered at the bottom of the cliff in the same spot where his friend's had been recovered years earlier. Had the black dog shown up for the third time?

DELAWARE
A SPIRIT NOT TO BE SNEEZED AT

Achew! Achew! Samuel Chew heard the snickering behind him and grimaced. He forced his eyes forward and continued down the cobblestone street. He was the Chief Justice of Delaware, an important man in the colony. But the mocking of his last name hurt as much as it had when he was a child. Surely, after all this time, the townspeople couldn't still think it was funny to pretend to chew loudly, mimic sneezes or wave a handkerchief as he walked by. He wished they understood how much it upset him. Someday, he vowed, he would teach them a lesson.

The thing was, people really did like and respect Samuel Chew. He was known as a smart and fair judge. When he died in 1743, he was mourned but some people continued to sneeze after saying his name. Samuel's spirit was fed up. The time had come, he decided. He began to haunt them.

The first to see his ghost was a farmer in Dover, who had been one of the loudest of the sneezers. Just as the sun set behind the barn one night, Samuel materialized. He was dressed in a judge's robe and white powdered wig.

Samuel haunted all who had teased him.

The farmer let out a cry of fright and Samuel chased him through fields, his black robes flapping in the wind. Finally, Samuel grew bored and let the farmer escape to the safety of his house.

Over that year, Samuel haunted all who had teased him. Many reported a tugging on their coat as they walked. But when they turned, no one was there. They'd continue on, and Samuel's ghostly hand would pull them back again and again. Sometimes, to give them a good fright, Samuel would show himself.

The townspeople were petrified. No one left their house after dark. Shops closed. Children were kept indoors. But they knew they couldn't live like this forever, so they gathered for a town meeting. They had to get rid of Samuel Chew's ghost. But how? A lot of solutions were offered, and they finally agreed to hold a funeral. Yes, they had already had a funeral for Samuel, but this funeral would be for his ghost! The next day, the townspeople arrived dressed in black and buried an empty casket. They said nice things about Samuel. No one sneezed. After that, Samuel seemed to stop his haunting. But his ghost will return if you dare to make fun of his name!

FLORIDA
HOME SWEET HAUNTED HOME

Attention, please! Paula's ghost is in the building. What building? Villa Paula, of course. If a majestic building had your name carved in big letters above the front door, wouldn't you hang around and haunt it too? Not in a scary way, but in an I-love-my-home kind of way.

Paula's Villa is located in what is now the Little Haiti neighborhood of Miami. It was built in 1926 by the Cuban government as a consulate—a place where foreign government officials work. The white stucco villa had high ceilings, tall windows, big chandeliers, and a lush garden. All the materials were shipped over from Cuba, and it was constructed by Cuban craftspeople. When it was completed, consul Don Domingo Milord and his wife Paula, who had been an opera singer, moved in. Domingo named the villa for Paula. Paula loved her beautiful home! She invited musicians and artists to perform and threw fabulous parties. She filled the rooms with colorful flowers from her garden and served her guests fresh-brewed Cuban coffee.

But six years later, Paula died from an infection. Domingo moved to Key West, and Paula? Well, many believe her spirit never left the villa. For years, the grand building sat abandoned. In the 1970s, a new owner set about restoring it to its former glory—and said he saw Paula's ghost floating down the hallway! He also heard the click, clack of her high-heel shoes on the villa's tile floors. Visitors reported smelling the strong scent of roses and coffee, when no flowers or coffee were anywhere in the house.

Many believe her spirit never left the villa.

The villa has since been a museum, fashion studio, and art gallery. An artist who worked there told that one day, a woman came in and introduced herself as a medium with the ability to talk to the dead. As she walked around, she found herself channeling Paula's spirit. She told the artist that Paula wanted the new owners to know how much the villa meant to her and how glad she was to see it lovingly restored. What a sweet and spooky thank you!

GEORGIA
WHAT LIES BENEATH

Phantom arms reaching up to grab swimmers. Restless spirits trapped far beneath the surface. Church bells chiming from the depths. A ghostly woman in a flowing blue dress wandering at night. Boats mysteriously careening and crashing. These are only some of the spine-chilling tales told of Lake Lanier, a large lake in the foothills of the north Georgia mountains.

Before the 1950s, there was no lake. The fertile valley was filled with oaks and hickories and dotted with small towns, like Oscarville. The U.S. Army Corps of Engineers decided to create a lake to bring water and electric power to Atlanta and surrounding counties and to provide protection from floods. The government paid about 700 families living in the area to move. Not moving wasn't an option. Houses, mills, and churches were demolished. Trees were uprooted. The nearby Chattahoochee River was dammed, and soon the land filled with water, burying the communities forever. Today, Lake Lanier contains enough water to fill almost one million Olympic-sized swimming pools!

Over eleven million people enjoy the lake each year, making it one of the most visited human-made lakes in the nation. But it's also one of the most dangerous. Divers have discovered submerged buildings, streets, and bridges at the bottom of the lake. Many complain this has made the murky water a treacherous obstacle course. But some blame underwater cemeteries. Before the lake was created, unmarked graves in small family plots were probably not moved. Could damp and disgruntled ghosts be haunting the lake?

Could damp and disgruntled ghosts be haunting the lake?

And what about the Lady of the Lake? One story goes that one night in 1958, a young woman named Susie was driving across the Lake Lanier bridge with her friend Delia May. Susie lost control of the car and it tumbled into the lake. The car sank, and the two women drowned. Delia's body was found, but not the car or Susie. For decades after, a ghostly woman in a blue dress was seen wandering near the bridge at night. Thirty-one years after the accident, the car was discovered and pulled out of the lake. Susie was given a proper burial.

HAWAII
THE NIGHT MARCHERS

Rump-a-thump-thump. The steady drumbeats in the middle of the night startled the family awake. A trumpeting of conch shells and the chanting of voices joined the rhythm. As the sounds grew louder, the family hurried outside onto the porch. They couldn't see anything. Then they heard the pounding of hundreds of approaching footsteps. "Get down!" the parents cried, making sure their kids lay face-down, flat on the floor. "The Night Marchers are coming."

The Night Marchers, or the Huaka'i Pō, are among the best-known legends on the eight islands that make up the state of Hawaii. The Night Marchers are the ghosts of ancient warriors whose job was to protect the ali'i, or chiefs. In life, the warriors would march ahead of the high-ranking chiefs to ensure their safety and clear the common people off the path. Traditionally, it is believed that these warriors still do their job in the afterlife. The phantom army journeys from mountain to ocean during certain phases of the moon. They're most often seen around sacred sites or where battles took place.

The trail of the Night Marchers has remained the same for generations. If your house, your school, or a store now stands in the way, they'll go right through the building! With thunderous drumbeats, the Night Marchers announce their arrival to give you plenty of time to hurry out of the way. Then the band of shadowy warriors appears, marching in step and carrying flaming torches. If you missed the warnings and the marchers are bearing down, you must lie on your belly and stay motionless to show your respect. And, whatever you do, keep your gaze down or your eyes shut. If you make eye contact, it's said they will sweep you away into the spirit world and you'll forever join their ranks as a Night Marcher!

> The phantom army journeys from mountain to ocean.

However, if your relative or ancestor happens to be in the procession, they will step forward and claim you as family, and your life will be spared. It doesn't need to be a close relative—a third cousin or a great-great-great aunt will do. Family gets a free pass!

IDAHO
RUN LIKE THE WIND

he boom of thunder startled the rancher awake. She couldn't believe it was storming again. The rain in Owyhee County had been heavy all week. She closed her eyes, letting the steady rhythm of the rain on the roof lull her back to sleep. Then came the faint whinny of horses from the barn. She bolted upright. Something was wrong.

Pulling on boots and a slicker, the rancher raced outside. The whipping wind plastered her hair to her cheeks, as a jagged bolt of lightning illuminated the sky. She saw water surrounding the barn. The Snake River must have flooded the valley! The rancher needed to get her horses to the safety of higher ground. But the barn door refused to open against the force of the rising water. Of all the nights for her family to be away visiting her relatives . . . She was alone and needed help. As she tugged on the door, she looked to the sky. To her amazement, the clouds began to swirl and churn. They picked up speed, moving faster and faster. Dawn broke, the wind stopped and the rain slowed. Then the clouds parted—and a majestic herd of ghostly horses emerged! The translucent mustangs had shimmering manes made of wispy clouds. Led by a white stallion, they galloped across the sky.

At that moment, the barn door released. The rancher rushed inside to find her three horses standing, terrified, in knee-deep water. She tried desperately to move them, but each time they reared up in fear. Outside, the herd of phantom mustangs silently touched down. Their otherworldly presence seemed to soothe the horses in the barn. They now let the rancher guide them into a paddock on a hill, away from the flood waters. Once the final horse was brought to safety, the spirit mustangs rose up in a line behind the stallion. They cantered in a circle, before being folded back into the clouds.

This tale is inspired by a legend from Owyhee County about a herd of spectral horses that lives in the clouds. The phantom mustangs are believed to magically materialize whenever a rancher or cowhand needs help. They've also been said to appear when someone is lost and alone in the rugged wilderness, to lead them to safety. Hundreds of living mustangs run wild in the canyon lands of Owyhee County, as well as in other parts of Idaho. Maybe the helpful spirit horses are descended from them?

Led by a white stallion, they galloped across the sky.

ILLINOIS
THE SPOOKTACULAR ZOO

In the women's restroom in Chicago's Lincoln Park Zoo, the visitor washed her hands then rummaged in her bag for a tube of lipstick. Checking her reflection in the mirror, she startled. A woman in a puffed-sleeve Victorian-era dress and a feathered hat stood right behind her, just an inch away. The visitor whirled around, but no one was there. She checked the entire restroom, opening every stall. Completely empty.

For more than 150 years, people have reported ghosts at the zoo. Human ghosts, that is. Not animals. They've been spotted in the mirror of this same bathroom many times. A woman in old-fashioned clothing is said to wander near the Lion's House, now called the Pepper Family Wildlife Center, oblivious to the modern-day visitors around her. Other ghosts reportedly appear and disappear quickly.

> Lincoln Park Zoo was built directly over the old cemetery.

Lincoln Park Zoo is one of the oldest in the country and, supposedly, the most haunted. Why? The land it sits on was once the Chicago City Cemetery. Built in the 1840s, this cemetery was the final resting place for around 30,000 people. Many had died from cholera, a disease caused by bacteria in contaminated water. Chicago residents were worried about all these bodies buried so close to Lake Michigan, the city's main water supply. So in 1866, the city closed the cemetery.

Families moved their dead relatives' graves. Then the Great Chicago Fire broke out. The historic blaze burned for three days in 1871, scorching over three square miles of the city, including the cemetery. The wooden markers on the graves not yet claimed—anywhere from 1,000 to 12,000—went up in flames, so they were never able to be identified.

Lincoln Park Zoo was built directly over the old cemetery. And what happens when cemeteries are moved but some bodies are left behind? Hauntings!

INDIANA
THE HAUNTED LIBRARY

The young boy barreled into the library, excited to choose his weekly pile of storybooks. In the doorway of the children's room, he stopped suddenly and pointed toward the shelves. "That lady!" he whispered. His mother looked about, confused. The only person here was a young librarian, who sat on the opposite side of the room. "That lady," the boy repeated. He told his mother she wore an old-fashioned long gray dress and a gray shawl. Overhearing him, the librarian called out. "Oh, your son can see our ghost!"

The poltergeist that haunts Willard Library in Evansville is known as the Grey Lady. In 1876, real estate and railroad mogul Willard Carpenter began building the library but died before it was completed. His children were furious when they learned that he'd left his fortune not to them but to the library. His daughter Louise sued to get their inheritance back, but lost. Decades went by and Louise died too, but the library continued to flourish. One cold winter morning in the 1930s, the library's janitor went down to the basement to check on the furnace. In the beam of his flashlight, a woman in a long gray dress and shawl appeared. Then she slowly faded away. The janitor fled in fear, and not long after, quit. The reason? He kept seeing this same ghost!

Books are found pulled from the shelves or oddly reordered.

He wasn't the only one. Over the years, staff and patrons have spotted what's believed to be Louise's spirit wandering the halls, checking up on her family's library. People have reported the chilling sensation of a ghostly hand resting on their shoulder or touching their hair. The sweet scent of lilac perfume is often heavy in the air when she's around. Books are found pulled from the shelves or oddly reordered, as if she were teasing the librarians.

The Grey Lady seems to still actively haunt the library. In fact, several GhostCams are set up around the library, and if you go onto their website, you just might catch a glimpse of her for yourself.

IOWA
THE GHOST WHO LOVES CHOCOLATE

A crescent moon hung low in the cloudy sky on that dark Iowa night. The two kids should have been asleep in their beds. Instead, they walked with forced swagger, both pretending to be braver than they truly felt. They'd been planning this secret experiment all summer, each sure the other would chicken out before they'd made it here. But neither had. Now they had reached the haunted bridge. The girl flicked on her flashlight, illuminating the Marsh Rainbow Arch Bridge that spanned the North Raccoon River. A soft breeze rustled the trees. The boy shivered then zipped his hoodie. Midnight was only minutes away. They broke into a jog.

The double-arched bridge south of Lake City was built in 1914, in a time of horse-drawn carts. Today, vehicles aren't allowed to cross it. In the middle of the bridge, the girl swung the flashlight from one end to the other and back again. No cars, no people, no animals. The boy solemnly slid a chocolate bar from his pocket. Gold foil glinted along the edges of the crisp red-and-blue wrapper. The girl lifted her wrist. The hands on her watch moved together to meet on the twelve. Midnight!

Slowly, they approached the chocolate bar— and gasped.

The boy placed the chocolate bar on the ground, in the exact middle of the bridge. They stared at it for a moment then hurried away, their sneakers thudding the pavement. Safely off the bridge, they ducked behind a tree. The girl clicked off the flashlight, allowing the darkness to blanket them.

Five minutes. The legends all said they had to wait for five minutes. They craned to listen but weren't quite sure what they were expecting. Footsteps? A gush of wind? The only sound was the distant hoot of an owl and the croak of nearby frogs. The girl checked her watch. The boy rocked on his heels. When the full five minutes had passed, they nodded nervously and headed back onto the bridge. Slowly, they approached the chocolate bar—and gasped.

The wrapper lay unopened. It was not ripped or wrinkled in any way, but the chocolate inside was gone! Vanished. The chocolate-loving ghost had been here and eaten it! They whirled about, searching for the friendly spirit. But, just as the legends said, it had materialized, eaten the offered chocolate at midnight then disappeared. Sweet *and* spooky!

KANSAS
THE BLUE LIGHT LADY

Some nights if you look beyond the tall prairie grass and up on a far-off hill, you may spot a hazy, blue light. That's not just any light—it's a glowing ghost known as the Blue Light Lady.

The legend of the Blue Light Lady started in the 1860s, when Elizabeth Polly and her husband Ephraim, a hospital steward, came to Fort Hays, an Army post in northwestern Kansas. They were at the frontier fort when a cholera epidemic hit. It wasn't understood then that the disease was caused by bacteria and spread by unclean water and contaminated food. Hygiene at the fort was poor, and hundreds of soldiers got sick.

It's unknown whether Elizabeth had formal nursing training, but working side-by-side with her husband, she tended patients around the clock. It's said they called her the "angel of the fort." The only breaks Elizabeth took were evening walks to nearby Sentinel Hill. The hill became her favorite spot, a peaceful escape from the sadness of the sick beds. Cholera is contagious, and Elizabeth caught the disease. She knew she was dying and made a final wish: to be buried atop Sentinel Hill. Elizabeth was given a military funeral and laid to rest in her blue dress and white bonnet. But the grieving soldiers discovered they couldn't dig into the hill's solid rock. Instead, they buried her down at the bottom.

It's said they called her the "angel of the fort."

Locals have since seen her ghost walking along Sentinel Hill, surrounded by a hazy blue light. In 1917, a farmer claimed a woman wearing a blue dress crossed his field and went into his shed. When he looked inside, no one was there. In the 1950s, a police officer feared he had accidentally run over a woman in a long blue dress on a road near the hill. But when he got out of his patrol car, no one was there.

After Fort Hays closed, the graves were moved but possibily not Elizabeth's. A memorial for her now stands atop the hill and there's a statue of her in town, but even so the Blue Light Lady continues her haunting.

KENTUCKY
SPIRIT OF A SPELUNKER

Imagine you're way down deep in one of Kentucky's underground tunnels. Suddenly you stumble on the uneven rock. But, before you fall, a ghostly hand grabs hold to steady you. Many believe it's the spirit of Floyd Collins, the state's greatest cave explorer, who helps those in danger.

Born in a log cabin in south-central Kentucky, Floyd spent his childhood spelunking, or exploring, the many interconnected tunnels and caves below the area's farms. Now called Mammoth Cave National Park, this 330-mile cave system is believed to be the longest in the world.

Not only was Floyd hurt, he was trapped in total darkness.

In January 1925, Floyd went sixty feet underground in Sand Cave. Holding a kerosene lamp, he dropped into a narrow hole, shimmied along tight corkscrewing passages, and launched feet-first into a pit of jagged rocks. He scrunched into a small horizontal space and—yikes!—his foot knocked over the lamp. An avalanche of small rocks rained down around him. Then a boulder landed on his leg. Not only was Floyd hurt, he was trapped in total darkness.

Days of failed rescue attempts followed. Meanwhile, an interview with Floyd done by a reporter who'd crawled part way in was shared around the nation via the new invention of radio. Thousands of people traveled to the cave entrance. Vendors sold hamburgers and souvenirs, as if it were a carnival, while inside, Floyd grew weaker. By the time rescuers reached him, Floyd was dead. He was buried in the family cemetery with a tombstone that read: "Greatest Cave Explorer Ever Known." And that should have been the ending to this sad story.

But a few years later, the cave was sold. The new owner dug up Floyd's body and displayed it inside Crystal Cave, another cave that Floyd had discovered. For decades, tourists paid to stare at Floyd's corpse, which lay in a coffin with a glass window. When the U.S. government eventually purchased Crystal Cave, Floyd's body was reburied in the cemetery. But, with everything that happened to this guy, you can see why his spirit may still be stuck down in the cave.

LOUISIANA
FOREVER GUESTS

The elevator opened onto the sixth floor, and a family stepped out. The parents didn't notice the girl in the black dress and white pinafore run past. But their son did. He'd spotted her several times since checking into the fancy hotel. She was always chasing a ball down this same carpeted hallway, never inviting him to join. He was hopeful now, as she turned in his direction. Then, to his amazement, he realized he could see through her. Her body and the ball faded in and out, in and out. She wasn't alive. She was a ghost!

Welcome to the Bourbon Orleans Hotel, one of the most haunted hotels in the country. More than twenty different spirits are said to be forever guests. Considering that this historic hotel in New Orleans' French Quarter has had quite the storied past, it's no surprise it's haunted.

> More than twenty different spirits are said to be forever guests.

The building first opened as the Orleans Theatre and Ballroom in 1815. Opera was performed on the stage, and Creole socialites attended glamorous masquerade balls under the sparkling chandeliers of the grand ballroom. After a destructive fire, the ballroom was purchased by the Sisters of the Holy Family in 1881. Founded by Henriette DeLille, they were one of the first Black orders of Catholic nuns in the United States. The nuns turned the ballroom into a convent and a school for girls, and later, an orphanage. During this time, yellow fever swept through New Orleans. The terrible sickness took the lives of several children and nuns.

The nuns sold the building in the 1960s, and it became a hotel. The elegant ballroom was restored to its former glory. Which brings us to today, and all the ghosts. The ballroom seems to be the biggest paranormal hotspot. A woman in a long, swishing gown has often been seen dancing there with an imaginary partner. The little ghost girl rolls her ball and chases it down the sixth floor corridors. Other girls have been seen napping in beds and the laughter of ghostly children has been heard. And it's said a phantom nun will swat a guest's knuckles if they get out of line!

MAINE
DON'T MOOSE WITH ME!

The trees in Maine's vast North Woods can feel endless. They blanket thousands of acres and reach so high, you often can't see the sky. Throughout the forested wilderness, you'll encounter plenty of animals, including black bears, white-tailed deer, foxes, and of course, moose. But have you ever heard of the enormous, ghostly-white moose said to haunt the woods' darkest corners? It's known as the Specter Moose.

In the 1890s, a man was out hunting near Lobster Lake when, through the tall trees, he spotted an immense moose. The animal looked as if it weighed close to 2,500 pounds. That's about the same weight as a small car! The hunter crouched low and silently edged closer. When he had the moose completely in sight, he stifled a gasp of disbelief. Its antlers stretched almost twelve feet across, and he counted twenty-two points on them! And the moose was completely light gray. The hunter took aim . . . but the bullet bounced off the moose!

The hunter tried again. The moose didn't flinch. It was as if the creature were invincible. The moose then let out an otherworldly roar. Pine needles rained down from the branches and birds took flight. The hunter stumbled backward in terror. Would the mighty creature charge? But the moose stalked away, quietly disappearing into the thick forest.

It was as if the creature were invincible.

Over the next century, other hunters attempted to bring down the moose, but none could. One group claimed to have killed the magical moose. They said they had strung it up in their camp before going to sleep. When they awoke in the morning, the moose was alive again! It stood on the edge of their camp, glaring at them with icy eyes. Then it ambled away.

Is the Specter Moose a supernatural creature that guards the North Woods? Or is it a very large white moose whose size was exaggerated by hunters? It's hard to know. White fur can occur in animals with a genetic mutation that causes a lack of pigmentation. Some Indigenous communities consider a white moose lucky. Whatever the Specter Moose may be, it's wise to pay attention when you're in the Maine wilderness.

43

MARYLAND
LEGEND OF BLUE DOG

isten closely late at night in the historic village of Port Tobacco, and you just may hear the haunting howl of a ghostly hound. The spooky legend of Blue Dog has been frightening folks since colonial times, making the tale as old as the United States itself.

The story starts with Charles Thomas Sims and his Bluetick Coonhound that everyone now calls "Blue Dog." Blue Dog adored Charles, and Charles adored Blue Dog. On the night of February 8th in an unknown year in the late 1700s, Charles entered a local tavern with Blue Dog. Charles was known for bragging and embellishing his stories. As the night wore on, he boasted about having a big bag of gold. Some of the patrons doubted him, but then Charles pulled the bag from his coat pocket. He held up the gold for all to admire. Across the tavern, Henry Hanos gaped greedily at the fortune.

Charles and Blue Dog left later that night. Unbeknownst to them, Henry slipped out too and silently followed the pair down Rose Hill Road. In the darkness, he overtook Charles and tried to rob him. But Charles fought back. The men struggled. That's when Blue Dog pounced on Henry. The force of his

heavy paws caused both men to stumble. Charles lost his balance and fell backward, smacking his head on a rock. He died instantly. Blue Dog bared his teeth menacingly, but the valiant dog met a tragic end at the hands of Henry.

Blue Dog adored Charles, and Charles adored Blue Dog.

Henry buried the gold under a tree. He'd come back for it when the coast was clear. Three days passed, and no one seemed to suspect him. Shovel in hand, he returned to the tree. But this time, someone was there. Someone very angry. Someone who wanted revenge. The ghost of Blue Dog. Forever faithful, the four-legged phantom refused to let Henry anywhere near the buried treasure. He growled and howled then lunged. Henry was so petrified that not only did he flee but he was still quaking the next day. He grew ill and literally died of fright.

For centuries after, locals have claimed that on February 8th, the anniversary of the robbery, Blue Dog can be heard howling by the tree. Supposedly the gold remains buried there. Are you brave enough to go treasure hunting and discover if the terrifying tale is true?

MASSACHUSETTS
PUKWUDGIES ARE WATCHING

he boys hiked through a dark, leafy forest in southeastern Massachusetts, telling jokes and enjoying nature. The hushed silence was broken only by the chirping of birds and their occasional laughter. Suddenly, a chill ran through their veins, stopping them in their tracks. They felt as if they were being watched. They scanned the trees and the underbrush. No other people. No big animals. And yet, deep in their bones, both sensed they were not alone. "Is a pukwudgie hiding nearby?" one boy whispered to the other. They started to run.

Have you ever heard of these ancient, magical woodland creatures? Pukwudgies are described as being two or three feet tall, or about the height of a toddler. They have smooth gray skin, glossy hair all over their bodies, and beady eyes that glow eerily in the shadows. Their noses, ears, and fingers are extremely large, and they walk upright. From the back, pukwudgies look like porcupines. From the front, they look liked trolls or goblins.

Pukwudgies are woven into the folklore of the Wampanoag Nation, who have long called Massachusetts home. It's told that the creatures were once friendly, but when the Wampanoag started to pay more attention to the giant Maushop, the mythical creator of Cape Cod, the pukwudgies became jealous. The little creatures started making life miserable, so Maushop banished them. But the pukwudgies came back . . . for revenge.

According to the legends, pukwudgies will shoot fiery arrows or conjure a mystical fire orb to lure a person deep into woods, never to return. They can even cause harm by just staring at you. And that's not all! Pukwudgies are said to possess the power to turn invisible, control the spirits of the dead, and shapeshift into dangerous animals, like cougars.

Pukwudgies are woven into the folklore of the Wampanoag Nation . . .

One woman said she was walking her dog in the forest when she noticed a small, gray creature with glowing green eyes watching her. The dog lunged, and the pukwudgie slunk away. Or so the woman thought. That night she awoke to find it tapping at her bedroom window. How scary! Luckily, it soon disappeared.

MICHIGAN
LAKE MONSTERS ON THE PROWL

When the sun shines bright on the thousands of lakes that dot Michigan, friends and families are found boating, waterskiing, fishing, and swimming. Up on the glimmering surface, it's fun and games, but what about down below in the dark, frigid waters? Anything could be lurking near the bottom of these incredibly deep lakes—even the most massive, fantastical beasts!

For centuries, strange creatures have been reported in the Great Lakes. The Anishinaabe, Odawa, Ojibwe, and Potawatomi people told stories of a Mishipeshu, or an underwater lynx, that lived in the lakes. Over the last hundred or so years, a colossal creature has been glimpsed swimming in icy Lake Superior. Named Pressie after the Presque Isle River, it has a blackish-green serpent's body, gleaming scales, a horse's head, a whale's tail, an extremely long neck, and measures 75 feet long—that's like lining up thirteen of your beds! Pressie appears to be harmless but curious. It enjoys chasing boats and sometimes will give one a playful nudge—hold on if you're on board!

> For centuries, strange creatures have been reported in the Great Lakes.

Over in the deep waters of Torch Lake, a creature with the head of a cat and the body of an enormous lizard covered in slimy green goo is rumored to swim. In Higgins Lake, tales are told of a yellow reptilian creature with sharp, bony spikes. And Lake Leelanau is home to a creature that disguises itself as a drifting log or tree. A teenager once rowed his rowboat into a marshy inlet to go perch fishing. He was tying his anchor rope to a dead cedar tree jutting out from the water, when two enormous eyes popped open! A creature with bark-like skin stared at him. As the kid let out a scream, it dove into the water. The creature's powerful tail propelled it into the center of the lake, where its head momentarily splashed to the surface before disappearing.

No one has ever been able to capture more than just a blurry photo of any of these beasts. Skeptics believe these creatures are really northern pike, muskellunge, or lake sturgeon that grew so huge they were mistaken for ancient monsters. What do you think?

MINNESOTA
GRAVE SECRETS

Two kids followed their mom out of the car and into the small, quiet cemetery. They'd been driving down a remote Minnesota road when she'd pulled over, insisting it would be fun to see the old graves. The kids didn't think moss-covered tombstones qualified as fun. But Mom was already inspecting the worn epitaphs etched onto the stones.

> *They both stopped, each overcome by the creepy feeling they were being watched.*

Sighing, they wandered toward the back corner. The cemetery was giving off majorly spooky vibes that fall night. Cornfields stretched out in every direction, and clouds drifting across the moon caused shadows to dance on the gravestones. Skeletal branches reached claw-like into the sky, as the kids' sneakers crunched on fallen leaves. Then they both stopped, each overcome by the creepy feeling they were being watched. And that's when they saw him. A small boy peering over a gravestone. His eyes wide, his mouth open, his body translucent. He darted from gravestone to gravestone, playing a ghostly game of hide-and-go-seek. When they called out, he disappeared completely.

According to local legend, the kids had met the ghostly boy who haunts the Ferguson Cemetery, located near the town of Norwood Young America. He's been seen peeking out from the tombstones and sometimes has a ghost dog with him. Many of the graves in the cemetery date back to the 1800s, when German and Swedish farmers first arrived in the area. Since several young boys are buried here, no one knows who the ghost is. However, many wonder if the one unmarked grave that stands by itself in the southwest corner may belong to the ghost.

And if this spirit boy isn't spooky enough, this final resting place has another legend. It's said that if you visit after midnight and count the number of trees at the center of the cemetery, then go over to the boy's grave, turn around and walk back to the center, there will be a different number of trees!

MISSISSIPPI
DEAD MEN TELL NO TALES

Right off the coast of Biloxi sits a small uninhabited island, called Deer Island. Today, it is mainly a breeding ground for the great blue heron. Wait, correction. It seems this marshy island may have someone on it, after all. Or does it not count if the person is no longer alive?

The haunting legend of Deer Island goes back to the early 1800s, when a pair of fishermen rowed up after a day of reeling in flounder from the Mississippi Sound. They decided to spend the night and set about making camp on the white-sandy shore. As the sun set, they built a campfire and roasted fish over its flames. Then they heard the rustling. They glanced at the nearby palmetto bushes. The fronds hung motionless, so it wasn't the wind. Probably wild hogs, they thought. But then the rustling grew louder. Now the men stood to investigate. They moved toward the bushes that were now shaking and, to their horror, out stepped . . . a headless skeleton!

They cried out in fear, as the skeleton took one step then another. Its bony arms reached for them. Hearts pounding, the men sprinted across the sand. The headless skeleton gave chase but the men ran faster. They managed to scramble into their boat and row across the bay to safety.

Its bony arms reached for them.

The next morning down by the docks, they shared what had happened. An old-timer told them that the skeleton was a dead pirate. Years before, a pirate ship had anchored by Deer Island. The captain had ordered his crew to bury their stolen treasure. Then he asked for a volunteer to watch over the booty. A young man new to the whole pirate thing said he'd do it, promising to guard it with his heart and soul. He didn't know this captain preferred his guards to be supernatural! The captain took out his cutlass, lopped off the young pirate's head, and left his body in the palmetto bushes. As he'd promised, the headless skeleton pirate has forever watched over the buried treasure, scaring away anyone who dares come too close. Now that's a terrifying security system!

MISSOURI
MOMO STINKS!

This frightening tale doesn't take place in the dark of night, but on a hot, sunny, summer afternoon in Missouri in 1972. Two brothers were outside playing with their dog. They lived in the town of Louisiana, on the banks of the mighty Mississippi River in the northeastern part of Missouri. Their back yard lay at the bottom of a hill covered by thick woods. The boys were running about with their dog, when a creature emerged from the trees.

The enormous creature was covered in shaggy, dark fur. It had a huge, pumpkin-shaped head with eyes that glowed bright orange. From where they stood, the brothers could smell the dank, foul odor wafting off its body. The older boy screamed so loud that his teenage sister peered out the bathroom window to see what was wrong. Her brothers grabbed the dog and raced inside. She bolted the door and telephoned her parents at work. When the police arrived, the creature was long gone. Search parties scoured the woods. They hung bait in trees to lure it out. But the Missouri Monster, or Momo, never appeared there again.

The enormous creature was covered in shaggy, dark fur.

Once word got out, two men from the nearby town of Troy came forward with their tale. Several months earlier, they said they had been out fishing on the Cuivre River, when a rotten-egg stench filled the air. One of the men clapped his hand over his nose. What was causing that gross odor? They heard a twig snap. On the opposite bank, they spotted what appeared to be a man with a beard and long hair shuffling along. They did a double take. The creature was way too tall and hairy to be a man, and its very large head seemed to rest directly on its shoulders. They ran as fast as they could for their car and sped away!

There were many other reported sightings of Momo during that summer. Some people found clumps of fur tangled in the branches of trees. One found a huge footprint with only three toes! Momo has not shown itself since the 1970s, and some now speculate that it was a bear mistaken for a creepy cryptid. Of course, a bear doesn't have three toes . . .

MONTANA
THE CRY OF THE HOMESICK BISON

he land that's now Montana once shook from millions of bison hoofs. The large, shaggy animals provided food for the Cree, Chippewa, Sioux, Assiniboine, Gros Ventre, Blackfeet, Crow, and Northern Cheyenne. Hides were turned into clothing and shelter. The bison's spirit brought peace, protection, and strength to the land's inhabitants.

There once sat a massive boulder in northern Montana, high on a ridge near the Cree Crossing overlooking the Milk River. It had been there for as long as anyone could remember. Scientists believe it was left behind by a glacier that once covered the region. The ancient, gray granite rock was special, because it looked like a sleeping bison with horns, a hump, and ribs. Many believed it held the same great power as the animal it resembled. Some touched the sleeping bison to bring good fortune before a hunt or battle. Having it watch over them was a source of comfort.

Then, in 1932, the U.S. government began to build Highway 2. The big boulder was in the way, so it was moved to a park in the town of Malta.

But as legend has it, the sacred rock was not happy about its new home. One night, residents were startled awake by bellows that sent shivers down their spines. It sounded like the anguished cries of a bull bison! The police searched ranches and livestock for the animal in pain, but the howls were finally traced to the park. As soon as the officers entered the park's gates, the bellows stopped. The next night they started up again. For days, months, and years the mournful cries continued on and off. Then the boulder in the park began to move—on its own! One inch. Then another. And another. It seemed as if the sleeping bison were slowly inching closer to the fence! Was it looking for a way out?

Residents were understandably upset. So, the boulder was moved once more and placed alongside the highway just outside the town of Saco. Today, people sometimes leave offerings to the stone beast, such as pennies, pictures, and flowers. And the bellowing appears to have stopped.

> The sacred rock was not happy about its new home.

NEBRASKA
THE MUSIC PLAYS ON

Listen closely in Centennial Hall, and you just may hear the haunting notes of a clarinet. The melancholy melody seems to come from the Music Room, yet there's never a musician in there. There are no speakers, no record players, no computers, and no woodwind instruments either. But that's because the eerie tune is being played by a ghost! And as we know, ghosts don't need to show themselves to give us goosebumps.

Centennial Hall is a museum in a small town called Valentine near the South Dakota border. It was a school long before becoming a museum. Built in 1897, it's believed to be the oldest high school building still standing in the Cornhusker State. Its halls were once filled with chattering students. Off to class. Off to lunch. Off to band practice. And it was in the music room, in 1944, that our story turned sinister.

Ghosts don't need to show themselves to give us goosebumps.

According to the legends, there was a girl who played the clarinet in the school band. She loved the clarinet's deep, warm sound and the way its melodies blended with those of the instruments around her. What exactly happened on that fateful day has been lost to time, but it seems that one of the reeds attached to her clarinet's mouthpiece had been dipped in poison. Was it by accident or on purpose? No one knows.

Either way, the clarinetist put the poisoned reed to her lips, ready to play, and met her end. Soon after she died, teachers began to report sightings of her ghost in the music room. Other students said they saw her apparition floating down the halls between classes, and whenever they entered the music room, they were overcome by a feeling of dread and unease. After the school was converted into a museum, the clarinetist's ghost remained in the building. Eerie music drifted out from the old music room, even though all instruments had been removed long ago. Some visitors have said they felt sick to their stomachs when they entered the room. Employees reported cold spots and a rocking chair that seemed to rock on its own. It's kind of like a ghostly game of musical chairs—except the music keeps on playing!

NEVADA
THE MERMAID'S REVENGE

Do you like stories about playful mermaids who sing happy songs while swimming with cute fish? Oh, well. This mermaid tale is quite the opposite. The mermaid who haunts Pyramid Lake is very angry and out for revenge.

Located in the northwestern part of the state, Pyramid Lake is a beautiful, glimmering lake in the desert. It gets its name from a pyramid-shaped rock in the center. The lake is the biggest and deepest remnant of the prehistoric Lake Lahontan, which covered much of Nevada millions of years ago. Because Pyramid Lake is so old, there's no telling what strange creatures lurk in its incredible depths, or in the case of our spiteful mermaid, up at the surface.

Calm water will suddenly froth and churn with no explanation.

For centuries, the Paiute people have lived in the area around the lake. The legend goes that one day a young Paiute man was wandering along the shore, when he heard a splash and spotted a mermaid. They started talking. The man returned day after day, and they laughed together and shared their deepest thoughts. Their friendship blossomed into true love. Soon after, the man lifted the mermaid out of the lake and carried her back to his village, so they could be properly married according to Paiute traditions. But when the tribal leaders saw her fish tail, they commanded him to return her to the lake. Much to the mermaid's shock and sadness, the young man did as he was told. He cast his true love back into the deep water.

She was heartbroken, but her sorrow soon turned to anger. The spurned mermaid placed a curse upon Pyramid Lake. She vowed that all Paiute people who came near its shores or swam in its waters would meet harm, and she promised to haunt the lake. Has she? Well, there have been reports that on sunny days, calm water will suddenly froth and churn with no explanation and then mysteriously stop. There have also been chilling stories of anglers who go out fishing and are never seen again. So if you do visit, never swim alone, and always keep your eyes open for a mermaid!

NEW HAMPSHIRE
THE WITCH WHO WASN'T

he Puritans who colonized New England feared witches above all else. They believed witches caused everything bad, from a devastating blizzard to a cow not giving milk to a slight toothache. Anything they couldn't explain, they blamed on the person they had decided was a witch.

Eunice Cole and her husband came to New Hampshire from England in 1638 as indentured servants. In exchange for their boat tickets, they had agreed to work for free for several years. Her husband sawed wood and, as far as we know, Eunice was a maid. The couple moved to the village of Hampton. They were childless and very poor, and Eunice was known to be grumpy and eccentric. All of this made her a target. Their neighbors began to whisper about Goody Cole ("goodwife" was the polite way to address women of low social standing, and it was usually shortened to Goody). They said she caused their cattle to get sick, put a curse on their crops, controlled the winds and made a fishing boat capsize. They said she was a witch.

As soon as she was freed, she was again accused of being a witch...

Goody Cole, or the Witch of Hampton as she was called, was put on trial. She cried out that she was innocent, but the jury did not believe her. No one in the town stood up to defend her. She was locked away in a cold, dark cell. After many years, she was allowed out of jail. But as soon as she was freed, she was again accused of being a witch and imprisoned. Goody Cole could not catch a break! By the time she was released, she was nearly 80 years old. She died soon after.

Fast forward to 1938. The town of Hampton was about to celebrate its 300th birthday, and its residents heard about the injustice put upon Goody Cole. They wanted to apologize for their ancestors' wrongful accusations. They planned a special celebration, officially cleared her of all charges, and burned copies of the court papers from her trials. But, it seems, Goody Cole wasn't having it. Soon after, the people of Hampton started seeing her ghost. A police officer said he once warned her to be careful on the uneven pavement. "I'll get along all right," she told him. "I've been walking these roads for hundreds of years." And then she vanished, as if by magic.

NEW JERSEY
THE PARKWAY PHANTOM

In the foggy darkness, the thrum of the car's engine and the rumble of the tires were slowly pulling the boy toward sleep. They'd started the drive to the Jersey shore late, because traffic on the Garden State Parkway was lighter at night. The boy fought the urge to close his eyes. Instead he pressed his nose to the window pane and peered out. There were no stores or businesses in sight. Just miles of highway edged by thick trees. Up ahead in the distance, he spotted a sign. They were approaching Exit 82 by the towns of Toms River and Seaside Heights. Then the boy did a double take. He sat straighter and squinted at the looming shadow. "Mom, look!" he cried.

The car's headlights illuminated an extremely tall man standing in the shoulder of the road. He wore a tan raincoat belted tightly around his narrow waist. A felt fedora pulled low over his brow hid his face in shadows. His arms were raised high above his head. They appeared to be absurdly long. Bending at both elbows, they moved back and forth in perfect rhythm, like windshield wipers or as if he were doing the Wave in a stadium.

The tall man had vanished.

"Should we help him?" the boy asked. His mom chewed her lip, considering. Then she slowed the car. "We're not getting out," she warned her son. "Just checking, okay?" He nodded nervously. They edged up to where he stood. But then he wasn't there. The boy looked over his shoulder. Had they driven too far? No. He wasn't anywhere in sight. The tall man had vanished!

Ever since the Garden State Parkway was completed in 1955, the Parkway Phantom has supposedly been sighted many times around this same stretch and always at night. He's also been called the Exit 82 Ghost. The state police have heard countless complaints about the specter. This section of the highway experiences many accidents due to speeding, and some officers wonder if the phantom's mission is to keep people safe by slowing down their cars. Talk about an otherworldly traffic patrol!

NEW MEXICO
A PARTY FOR THE DEAD

Are you ready to throw an epic welcome home party? Because along with fall breezes, November can blow in a whole bunch of ghosts! Día de los Muertos, or Day of the Dead, is a two-day celebration that takes place every year on November 1st and 2nd. It's a joyous occasion, when it's believed the souls of our ancestors visit families and friends.

To welcome and honor the dead, many families set up an ofrenda, or altar, in their homes. Pictures of loved ones are placed on a table or a fireplace mantel that's been decorated with real or paper cempasúchiles, or marigolds. Called flor de muerto, or flower of the dead, the marigolds' strong scent and brilliant orange color are said to help guide the spirits back home from the grave. Favorite foods are prepared, beverages poured, and cherished mementos displayed. Homes and gravesites are decorated with colorful calavera de azúcar, or sugar skulls, and tissue-paper papel picado banners. Many towns will have community ofrendas for all to take part in. Bakeries are filled with pan de muerto, a sweet bread shaped into skulls or bones.

Día de los Muertos may have started centuries ago in Mexico. To the Aztec, Toltec, and Nahua people, death was a natural part of the cycle of life. They believed it was important to keep a strong connection with family members who had passed away. But they thought being sad was disrespectful. Instead, they danced, feasted, and wore bright colors to celebrate them.

Revelers paint their faces to look like skulls...

Today, Día de los Muertos and other similar celebrations are enjoyed throughout the world, especially Central and South America and the southwestern United States. Some people stay home with family. Some have picnics at gravesites. Others dance in parades. In New Mexico, streets are decorated with marigolds, mariachi bands play, and mojigangas, traditional Mexican giant puppets, lead candle-lit walks. Revelers wear fancy costumes and paint their faces to look like skulls or La Catrina, the glamorous, jewelry-wearing skeleton.

On November 3rd, goodbyes are said, but they're not forever. In a year, the dead will return to celebrate all over again.

NEW YORK
SISTERS KEEPING COOL

Snowflakes swirled above the skaters circling Wollman Rink in Central Park. The majestic park is in the middle of bustling Manhattan and surrounded by towering skyscrapers. On this crisp winter night, kids lined up at a nearby cart to buy pretzels. Yellow taxis beeped in the distance. A group of friends linked hands as they happily glided around the outdoor rink. Their laughter rose above the beat of the music, and their blades etched grooves into the slick surface. Soon everyone was being ushered off so the Zamboni could clean the ice. Before heading to the snack bar one boy paused and glanced back over his shoulder. He blinked in disbelief. "Hey, look!" he cried, grabbing the jacket of the friend standing closest and pointing. The girl sucked in her breath. She saw it too.

Two phantom figure skaters, hand in hand, gliding in the center of the rink. One wore an old-fashioned red dress with a big bustle. The other wore the same style of dress but hers was purple. The kids watched in awe as the ghosts dreamily performed an endless series of figure eights. Their blades glided silently, never touching the surface of ice. The two young women seemed unaware of the other skaters darting about, and no one else saw them. They started to twirl.

The skating spirits are said to be Janet and Rosetta Van Der Voort, sisters who lived in Manhattan in the 1800s. Legend has it their wealthy parents were extremely overprotective. They rarely let the girls leave their apartment alone. The only place they allowed them to visit unaccompanied was the lake in Central Park to ice skate in the winter. The Van Der Voort sisters loved skating and they happily spent hours enjoying their freedom. They were best friends, and they spent their lives together. After one sister died of old age, the other died a few months later.

For over one hundred years, New Yorkers have reported the spirit sisters, decked out in Victorian clothing, figure skating in the park. Sometimes the pair circles Wollman Rink and sometimes they return to the lake, even though it no longer freezes over. It seems these ghosts can skate on water! They show up most often at night, and they've been sighted in both the winter and the summer. But don't be afraid of the park! These sisters aren't out to scare you—they just want to have an ice day.

Two phantom figure skaters, hand in hand, gliding in the center of the rink.

NORTH CAROLINA
THE BROWN MOUNTAIN LIGHTS

How long do you think people have witnessed the unexplained orbs of dancing light that sometimes appear over the Brown Mountain range in the western part of the state? A decade? A century? Try eight centuries! Legends of these mysterious lights are said to date back to the year 1200. Yet no one has ever figured out what they are.

The ghostly lights are usually seen on clear nights around the Linville Gorge area. They've been described as white, red, yellow, orange, or blue. Sometimes they're described as large luminous balls and other times as small pinpricks of light. They've been seen low to the ground and high in the sky. They've been spotted bobbing frantically and holding completely still until mysteriously extinguishing, as if a candle in the sky were blown out. Sometimes the lights hover for a while and other times they flash and go. Everyone seems to experience them differently, but they all wonder the same thing: what are they? What causes them?

> The ghostly lights are usually seen on clear nights around Linville Gorge.

There's been a lot of stories and guesses and even some scientific investigation. One ancient legend tells of a great battle between the Cherokee and Catawba, and that the lights are the spirits of lantern-carrying women searching for the fallen warriors. Land surveyors in the 1770s called them "some kind of luminous vapor," but that was scientifically proven false. In 1913, a U.S. Geological Survey concluded they were headlights from a train. But three years later, the tracks washed away and trains stopped chugging through the area, and people continued to see the lights. So that theory didn't hold up! Could they be car headlights? People have been seeing the lights since before cars were invented. Others have wondered if they could be caused by swamp gas, but there are no swamps around. Are they moon dogs, which is the term for moonlight shining on haze? Possibly, but the lights have been seen on moonless nights. How about foxfire, the light from decaying wood, insects, and animals? Also possible, although scientists have yet to prove this. And then there are those who speculate that the lights are caused by aliens or ghosts. Do you think we'll ever solve the mystery of the Brown Mountain Lights?

NORTH DAKOTA
THE HAPPY BIRTHDAY GHOST

When things get spooky in Medora, some locals blame the spirit of Teddy Roosevelt, the 26th president of the United States. The long-dead president looms large in the rugged Badlands, but other ghosts have also made themselves at home in this historic North Dakota town with its wooden sidewalks, stagecoach rides, and cowboys. A huge house may be haunted. A hotel claims to have resident ghosts. And there's a chilling visitor in the ice cream shop.

Located on the Little Missouri River, Medora was formed in 1883 by a French nobleman named Marquis de Mores. He named the town in honor of his wife, Medora von Hoffman. They built a chateau (that's French for a really big mansion). Today, the chateau is a museum. Some claim it's haunted by the spirit of a woman. They report seeing strange lights flicker on when no one is in the building and feeling unexplained cold spots. Is Medora doing the haunting? No one knows.

There have been reports of spooky cold spots.

Soon after the town was founded, a young Teddy Roosevelt arrived in the Dakota Territory for a hunting trip. He fell in love with the stark, wide-open prairies and majestic rock formations and became a rancher. His time here helped him understand the importance of preserving the nation's wilderness. But it's not his ghost who's hanging around. Hotel guests have reported seeing the spirit of a young boy in one of the top-floor rooms. They have awoken to sounds of children playing in the hallways only to find no one there. Some people have heard the sound of flushing toilets in empty bathrooms. Who are these ghost kids? Good question!

And then there's the Birthday Ghost. Some locals say that the Medora Fudge and Ice Cream Depot is haunted by the spirit of a woman who only appears once a year on her birthday. Luckily, she seems as sweet as the flavors being scooped. There have also been reports of spooky cold spots, but that's not weird for an ice cream store!

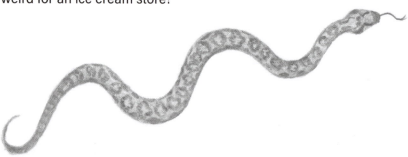

OHIO
RACER BOY

he cousins bumped fists as they piled into the first car of The Racer. They didn't agree on much but when it came to roller coasters, they both liked the front. Nothing beat seeing each terrifying drop and turn loom before them. They let out a whoop as the seat belts and lap bar locked in, and the red wooden coaster began to chug forward. On a parallel track, a blue coaster kept pace. The ride was a race between the Red Racer and Blue Racer, and the cousins leaned forward, hoping to propel their coaster to victory.

At the top of the first hill, they held their breath . . . and then in a whoosh, the coaster plummeted and their stomachs dropped to their toes. The coaster moved faster and faster, climbing up then hurtling down, banking bends and careening around curves. The ride began to slow as it entered a tunnel—oh, no! A boy was on the tracks! He wore a white shirt and pants and was walking along, unaware that a huge roller coaster was about to flatten him. The cousins waved their arms and screamed to get out of the way, but their calls were drowned out by the coaster's roar. It bore down upon him and then . . . the kid vanished.

Their calls were drowned out by the coaster's roar.

When the ride was over, the cousins grabbed the first park employee they saw, begging him to check the track. When he did, no one was there. The cousins had witnessed "Racer Boy," a spirit said to haunt Kings Island Amusement Park in Mason, Ohio. Legend has it a small boy dressed entirely in white sometimes appears just before sunset or after dark alongside the tracks or in the tunnel. Luckily, the ghost seems to be friendly.

When Kings Island opened in 1972, the 88-foot high wooden roller coaster was its signature attraction. It's rumored that two of its cars may have come from the old Shooting Star ride at Cincinnati's Coney Island amusement park. One theory is that the ghost of a boy who had fallen off the Shooting Star tagged along to Kings Island, and has haunted the coaster ever since.

OKLAHOMA
WE HAVE SPIRIT, YES WE DO!

The boisterous fans packed into the University of Oklahoma football stadium all raised their index fingers to the sky and chanted, "OH , oh, oh, oh, OOOOOOOOO!" Then the kicker sent the ball soaring toward the opposite end zone, and they cried out in unison, "U!" A dog joined in with a haunting *howooooool.* At least, that's what the two kids sitting in the first row thought they heard. They shifted their gaze away from the action to search the stands for the canine cheerleader. But they couldn't find a dog anywhere amid the sea of crimson and cream. Had they been wrong? Or was it the ghost of Mex, the former mascot, rooting for his home team?

A cute terrier was the first OU mascot. In 1914, an army field medic from Oklahoma found a stray dog while stationed along the Mexican border during the Mexican Revolution. He named the shaggy pup "Mex." Mex hung out with the medic unit and liked to cheer up the patients. The next year, when the medic returned home to attend University of Oklahoma, Mex came along. Mex sat by his side during class and became the football and baseball teams' loyal mascot. Mex took his mascoting job very seriously. On game days, he wore a crimson and cream sweater with a big letter "O" on the side and a matching cap. He would roam the sidelines to keep all stray dogs and other animals from wandering onto the field. (This was a problem back then!) The players taught Mex when to cheer. He'd bark at a touchdown, howl at a kick, and go woof for a homerun! He quickly became the team's lucky charm.

The phantom mascot still comes to all the home games.

Mex died of old age on April 30, 1928. He was so beloved that the university shut down for his funeral. Students and faculty gathered, as his small casket was lowered into a burial spot underneath the football field stadium. Today, no one knows exactly where that spot is. In the years that passed, the field has been renovated many times and a stadium built over it. But Mex's grave was never uncovered, so it must still be there, somewhere— which makes sense, since the phantom mascot still comes to all the home games. Both fans and athletes have reported feeling a little dog lick their fingers or snuggle up against their legs. But when they looked down, no dog was there. This dog is a forever fan!

OREGON
GHOST ON THE COAST

The college students huddled around a Ouija board. They'd all heard that the house next door to the Heceta Head Lighthouse in Yachats was haunted by the wife of a former light-keeper. Tonight, they were hoping to communicate with her.

Heceta Head Lighthouse sits atop a 1,000-foot-high forested cliff that overlooks the Pacific Ocean. In fog and the dark of night, its bright beam has warned sailors of the jagged rocks since 1894. Back then, the head light-keeper lived inside the lighthouse, and two assistant keepers and their families shared the house alongside. At some point, according to legend, the daughter of one of the assistant keepers drowned in the sea. Her parents moved away but after they died, it's said the mother's spirit returned to the lighthouse to keep eternal watch over her daughter.

Once the lighthouse became automated decades later, keepers weren't needed. That's when the house's caretakers began to hear unexplainable noises. In 1975, a worker was in the attic, cleaning the windows, and noticed an odd reflection in the glass. He turned . . . to see a misty woman in a long dark dress! He raced away in terror.

It's said the mother's spirit returned to the lighthouse.

A few days later, he was fixing the outside of the house when he accidentally broke an attic window. He boarded it up, leaving the shattered glass inside on the floor. No way was he going in there! That night the caretakers heard the sound of scraping coming from the attic. In the morning, they went up to investigate—and found the glass swept into a neat pile. And they were the only ones at home! Not long after, the college kids arrived and placed their fingertips on the Ouija board pointer. The candles in the room flickered. Their fingers moved as if guided by an unseen force. The board spelled out "R-U-E."

Years later, after the house was turned into a popular bed and breakfast, housekeepers reported feeling Rue's presence. After making a bed, they'd see a depression in the sheets, as if Rue had just sat down! One guest reported seeing a doorknob turn on its own and the door open by itself!

PENNSYLVANIA
AROUND AND AROUND SHE GOES

Have you ever ridden an old-fashioned carousel with colorful, carved animals and peppy organ music? When you scramble on, what's your first-choice animal? The pretty pony that goes up and down? The regal horse with the flowing mane? The fierce tiger or perhaps the silly seal? Mrs. Muller always chooses the black military horse. But she never has to race for it, like you might. Why's that? Mrs. Muller is a ghost!

The story starts in the early 1900s. Daniel Muller was a talented artist and sculptor, who is considered to be the greatest carver of carousel horses. From a block of wood, he'd create the most amazingly realistic and fantastical animals. His wife fell in love with a black military horse he carved. She called it "my horse" and was devastated when, in 1921, it was attached to a carousel and she had to say goodbye. The carousel traveled with carnivals from town to town until, in 1971, it was purchased by Cedar Point Amusement Park in Ohio. Mrs. Muller was long-dead by then, but that didn't stop her ghost from following her beloved horse to its new home.

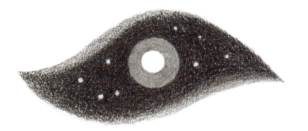

At night, when the park was dark, employees would report the carousel's lights mysteriously flicking on and the Wurlitzer organ music starting up. Mrs. Muller, they said, would sit astride her horse, eerily going around and around and around.

> Mrs. Muller would sit astride her horse, eerily going around and around…

In 1995, the Antique Carousel was moved to Dorney Park in Allentown, Pennsylvania, where it's the first ride through the amusement park's front gate. But Mrs. Muller's Military Horse didn't come with the carousel. It was put on display at a museum in Ohio. For whatever reason, Mrs. Muller decided museum life wasn't for her and traveled to Pennsylvania, too. According to stories, she can be seen after Dorney Park has closed for the night. The carousel, with its sixty-six carved animals and two chariots, will be dark and quiet. Then it suddenly whirs back to life without a living soul nearby, and her ghostly apparition appears. Cloaked in white, Mrs. Muller is the sole rider on the creepy carousel. Perched atop a phantom horse, she slowly spins as haunting melodies play. Care to climb aboard and keep her company?

RHODE ISLAND
THE HIGH-SOCIETY SPIRIT

If your family had a super-fancy mansion with a private beach on the Atlantic Ocean, you might want to hang out there all the time—maybe even in death. That's what Alice Vanderbilt seems to have chosen.

In America, the period from the late 1800s through 1929 was known as the Gilded Age. During this time a handful of families who'd made incredibly huge fortunes flaunted their wealth. Cornelius Vanderbilt constructed the nation's first railroads and steamships. After his death, a big chunk of his fortune (billions in today's money) was passed down to his grandson, Cornelius Vanderbilt II. Newport, Rhode Island was the go-to summer destination, so naturally Cornelius II and his wife Alice built a summer "cottage" in the City-by-the-Sea. They named it The Breakers. Their "cottage" had three floors, forty-eight bedrooms, a grand ballroom, formal gardens, an arcade, and was decorated with real gold, silver, and platinum. Think of the fanciest house you've ever seen—now multiply that by ten. Or one hundred. Get the picture?

Alice had seven children, but one of her daughters and four sons died before her. Her husband passed away unexpectedly in 1899. After that, Alice dressed only in black and never left home without a thick veil covering her face. When she died in 1934, she left the mansion to her youngest daughter, Gladys. Gladys leased it to the Preservation Society of Newport for $1 a year, so it could be shared with the public. But she had one condition—the family would always be allowed to live on the third floor. They still summer there today. And so does Alice's ghost.

They still summer there today. And so does Alice's ghost.

Since her death, Alice Vanderbilt's spirit has been sighted by family, employees, and visitors. She wears a long, old-fashioned dress and is said to roam near her bedroom. Sometimes the furniture has been found rearranged to how it was when she was alive! When a TV series was filmed in the house, the lead actress reported feeling Alice's presence beside her when she said her lines. Why is Alice still lingering? The Breakers was her happy place, where she felt most at peace.

SOUTH CAROLINA
A WARNING FROM BEYOND

When the weather is about to turn wild, Pawleys Island residents keep their eyes peeled for the Gray Man. If the legendary ghost appears, it's time to leave the barrier island—and fast. For two hundred years, this phantom forecaster has been sighted right before every major hurricane!

The Gray Man has been described as wearing a long gray overcoat and a gray hat. As storm clouds gather over the Lowcountry and the Atlantic Ocean churns, he patrols the island's windswept beaches and marshes. He will walk silently by some people but speak to others. "Leave," he warns. "Leave at once. You are in danger!" If you heed his warning, it's said you will return after the storm to discover your house undamaged. In fact, many who have claimed to see the Gray Man came back to find their house was the only one still standing on their block!

Many legends swirl around the Gray Man's origin. One of the more popular ones is a love story. Long ago, there was a nameless young man who had been traveling abroad and missing his fiancée something awful. She too was counting the days until they could be together. Finally, the man's ship docked in Charleston.

He made her promise to leave now—then disappeared.

He continued his journey on horseback, taking a shortcut through untraveled marsh just outside Pawleys Island. Thick pluff mud clung to his horse's legs, and the animal threw the man to the ground. The mud acted as a giant vacuum cleaner, sucking him down, down, down under the surface. The more he thrashed, the deeper he was pulled, until the earth swallowed him up.

After his funeral, his fiancée started taking solitary strolls along the beach to lift her sadness. One day as her hair blew about in a sudden gust, a figure dressed in gray approached. She let out a startled cry. It was him! But how? She started to question him, but he cut her off. He warned that a bad storm was blowing in. He made her promise to leave now—then disappeared.

The woman raced home and told her parents. They wasted no time packing their bags and heading inland. That night, a powerful hurricane with heavy winds and lashing rain roared ashore. It destroyed all the buildings on the island, except for one: her family's home. Ever since, the mysterious Gray Man has continued to keep residents safe from the fury of Mother Nature.

SOUTH DAKOTA
THE GHOSTLY FISHERMAN

The Black Hills of South Dakota are home to some of the country's best fishing waters. Here, you can reel in rainbow trout, largemouth bass, walleye, and northern pike. And in the shimmering Pactola Lake, just west of Rapid City, there are rumors of a phantom fisherman.

According to lore, there once was a local man who loved fishing. Every day, no matter the season or the weather, he cast his line into the water or drilled a hole into the ice. His story dates to before a dam created Pactola Lake. A small town used to be located where the lake now sits, and Rapid Creek ran alongside it. In the winter, this fisherman had no problem locating where the ice was thinnest. He would bore a hole and dangle a wet fly in the chilly water. Then he'd stand on the ice, or sit on an overturned bucket, and patiently wait for a brown trout to bite. One day without warning, *crack!* The ice beneath his feet began to spiderweb in all directions. Small cracks quickly turned to large cracks. There was no time to run before the ice gave way. He plunged into the frigid creek and drowned. The townspeople had to wait until the spring thaw to take his body out and properly bury him. And that should have been the end, until . . .

Many didn't realize he was no longer alive.

. . . anglers began to spot him once more. They saw him fishing up and down the creek. He looked so happy and lifelike that, at first, many didn't realize he was no longer alive. But no fish the phantom fisherman caught ever had a hook mark in its lip. Once the lake was created, anglers reported their ice fishing lines feeling like they were being grabbed away, then going limp. It felt less like the pull of a fish and more like the way a frantic person trapped under the water would tug. And then there was the eerie cracking noise. It seemed to start *underneath* the surface of the lake, as if someone were desperately trying to break free. It's said that if you drilled a hole in the ice large enough for a person to crawl through, the cracking stopped. But once the hole froze over, the cracking would start up again. A chilling tale, for reel!

TENNESSEE
THE PHANTOM OF THE ORPHEUM

he audience sat wide-eyed, watching the actors dance across the famous Orpheum Theatre's huge stage in downtown Memphis. They were at the funny part of the show, where one of the actors sang the song "Twinkle Twinkle Little Star" horribly off-key. But before the audience could erupt into laughter, a child's voice joined in, her eerie melody perfectly in tune. Confused, the actor whirled about. Who was singing? The sweet voice seemed to come from everywhere . . . and nowhere.

Everyone backstage searched for the mystery singer, but to no avail. The next night, the cast gathered nervously. Once again, the actor's solo strangely transformed into a duet. The unseen child sang as if she knew the song well. "That must be Mary," the staff at the Orpheum told the terrified actor. Mary is one of the theater's many resident ghosts.

Believed to have died in a trolley accident outside the theater in 1921, Mary has been haunting it ever since. She has been glimpsed dancing in the lobby to the music of the pipe organ, running up the aisles, and playing hide-and-go-seek. Performers have reported seeing a girl wearing a white, old-fashioned dress with black stockings and no shoes sitting in seat C-5 on the mezzanine level. This is Mary's favorite seat. People sitting near C-5 often find themselves shivering in her cold presence.

Mary seems to be friendly, although a little mischievous.

Mary seems to be friendly, although a little mischievous. In the musical *Annie*, Daddy Warbucks gives Annie a giant dollhouse. The dollhouse used on stage at the Orpheum was extremely heavy, needing two crew members to move it. Then one night it disappeared. The crew looked everywhere, until they finally found it . . . all the way up in the mezzanine, next to Mary's favorite seat!

TEXAS
THE FOREVER FIRE FIGHTER

The big bay door opened all on its own. The lights randomly flicked on then off. The firefighters at Fire Station No. 9 in El Paso didn't freak out. They knew what this meant—it was a supernatural head start! They quickly pulled on their gear, stepping into protective pants, zipping up heavy jackets, securing hard hats, boots, and gloves. When the fire alarm finally blared, their oxygen tanks were already on and they were climbing onto the trucks. It sure does help to have a long-dead fire captain haunting your fire station when there is a blaze to battle.

The fire forecaster is believed to be the ghost of Captain W. F. Bloxom. Bloxom loved fighting fires and hanging out with his crew at the station. One February day in 1934, when Bloxom was captain, an alarm sounded. A furniture warehouse across the street from the station had ignited.

The crew raced over and unfurled the hoses, training powerful streams of water on the fire. Even so, the scorching heat spread quickly. Black smoke billowed, making it hard to see. More crews were called in to help. Wasting no time, Captain Bloxom led a squad into the huge blazing building to double-check that no one was inside. The all-clear was given, but then suddenly the captain and two other firefighters found themselves trapped by a frightening wall of flames. They managed to rush through to safety but later, in the hospital, Captain Bloxom passed away from inhaling too much smoke.

The firefighters credit Captain Bloxom as the station's guardian angel.

Ever since then, the captain has haunted the fire station. Some firefighters have reported feeling his presence behind them as they climb the stairs. Others have felt a cold sensation, as if his ghost were passing through their bodies. Furniture has been found scattered about, perhaps being rearranged by the captain. One firefighter said he witnessed the water fountain go on, with the knob turning on its own.

Although he can be a bit of a prankster, the firefighters credit Captain Bloxom for acting as the station's guardian angel. Most times the unexplainable spookiness has occurred right before a call comes in. Speed is key when putting out fires, and because of his ghostly warnings, they can often reach the flames faster. It seems some first responders never stop protecting us!

UTAH
THE WEEPING STATUE

Have you ever seen a marble statue cry? In the Logan City Cemetery next to the Utah State University campus, there's a haunted statue that's said to weep real human tears! She's perched atop a tall stone, clutching a ring of flowers with one hand and resting her forehead in the other hand. Her shoulders slump with the incredible weight of her sadness. Why is this statue weeping?

The statue was carved in memory of a grieving woman named Julia Cronquist. Julia and her dairy-farmer husband Olif came to Utah from Denmark. They had eight children, but five of them tragically died in childhood between 1889 and 1901—all but one from outbreaks of scarlet fever. Losing her beloved children, one by one, was too much for Julia. Every single day, she would walk to the cemetery and sob over their graves. It seemed as if she would never stop crying. Julia had also had a bout of scarlet fever and was left with a weakened heart. This, combined with her emotional heartbreak, took its toll, and Julia died in 1914.

Her husband ordered a statue showing her overcome by grief and had it placed above her grave in the cemetery. The university surrounds the graveyard, so students often walk through on their way to and from classes. Over the years, there have been many stories about the statue and the tears it's said to shed. Some students say that if you stand in front of it at midnight and say, "Weep woman, weep," it will cry. Others say it must be at midnight during a full moon. Another legend says you must first make a circle around the statue with your friends, hold hands, and then chant "Weep woman, weep" for her to cry. And yet another version says she will only cry on the anniversaries of each of her children's deaths. Either way, students claim they have touched the Weeping Woman statue and felt wet tears rolling down her cheeks!

Have you ever seen a marble statue cry?

VERMONT
THE TAP-DANCING GHOST

All was quiet the night winter rolled into Vermont, blanketing the pine trees and roads with heavy snow. At the Green Mountain Inn in Stowe, the family in Room 302 opened the frosted window and reached out to touch the swirling flakes. Tomorrow was looking like a great ski day. *Tap, tap, tap.* The sound came from above. They gazed up at the ceiling. Was an animal on the roof? *Tap, tap, tap. Tap, slap, shuffle, tap.* The tapping seemed to have a rhythm. As if someone were tap dancing across the roof—in a snowstorm! Was that possible? Maybe so. The inn claims to have their own resident ghost—a tap dancer named Boots Berry. His story goes like this . . .

Boots Berry was born in the 1840s, possibly in what's now Room 302. Boots' parents both worked at the inn. His mom was a chambermaid and his dad tended the horses. Boots loved horses and became an accomplished rider.

Tap, slap, shuffle, tap.

When he was a young man, a group of stagecoach horses got spooked and bolted down the main street of their mountain village. Boots heroically hopped onto his horse and gave chase, single-handedly halting the runaway horses.

Boots eventually left Vermont and traveled south. Along the way, he got into trouble with the law. While in jail in New Orleans, a fellow prisoner taught Boots how to tap dance. *Clickety-clack.* Boots' fancy footwork became legendary and may be how he got the nickname "Boots." (No one remembers his real name.) After his release from jail, Boots returned to Vermont and the inn. He was there in 1902, when a fierce snowstorm blew in.

As the blizzard gusted, someone on the ground looked up and noticed a small girl stranded on the roof. She sat huddled, shivering from fright and cold. Boots raced to the attic and climbed out a window. He inched carefully across the roof's icy shingles until he reached the girl. He lowered her down to safety. Then his foot slipped and . . . he fell to his death. Ever since, it's been said that Boots' tap dancing can be heard on the inn's roof during snowstorms. And where do you think he was standing when he slipped? Right above Room 302!

VIRGINIA
THE TUNNEL VAMPIRE

ccording to local lore, a vampire slumbers in one of the crypts in the Hollywood Cemetery in Richmond. When the sun goes down, the fanged creature emerges to search for fresh blood to drink!

This story gets its spooky start on a cool, rainy afternoon in 1925. The nearby Church Hill train tunnel was undergoing repairs, and as a steam locomotive pulling ten flat cars passed through, the tunnel collapsed. The dirt walls caved in. Bricks tumbled down. The train was trapped under mounds of debris and rescuing the passengers and workers took many days. Fearing the tunnel would collapse even more, the state decided it was safest to seal it up for good.

Very soon after, a vampire is said to have appeared at the cemetery. He seems to live in a mausoleum belonging to a bookkeeper named William Wortham Pool. Pool was not on the train or part of the disaster. He'd died three years earlier of pneumonia. So why did the vampire choose his grave? Instead of his full name, Pool had just his initials "W. W." carved onto the stone mausoleum. What do the initials look like? Vampire fangs!

> They watched in horror, as it leaned ever closer to the victim's neck.

Some say the vampire may be Pool himself. Others believe he was one of the trapped workers. And there's a version of the legend that goes like this: the rescue team were digging the rubble out of the tunnel when they spotted a creature crouching over one of the victims. It was dressed in black and had pointed teeth. They watched in horror, as it leaned ever closer to the victim's neck. The rescuers cried out and the creature took off in a flash. The rescuers gave chase, but it was supernaturally fast. After crossing the James River, the creature darted into the hilly cemetery and disappeared into W. W. Pool's mausoleum, without ever prying open the sealed door. And that's where it still resides.

Of course, some people suggest that what the workers really saw was an injured person with broken teeth, who had staggered away from the tunnel, wandered into the cemetery, and been mistaken in the shadowy darkness for a vampire. What do you think? Is there a vampire in Richmond?

WASHINGTON
A SPECTRAL SHOPPING TRIP

Every day, thousands of visitors come to Pikes Place Market in downtown Seattle to eat delicious food, shop for farm-fresh fruits and flowers, watch fishmongers fling fish—and glimpse a ghost, or two, or fifty! This enormous market is said to be the most haunted place in the northwestern United States. There are too many ghosts lingering about to tell all their tales, so we'll introduce you to a few of our favorites.

Let's start at the magic shop. Several decades ago, an old woman wrapped in a purple shawl entered. She silently shuffled to the counter and handed a crystal ball to the owner. Then, without a word, she turned and disappeared into the market's crowded hallways. The owner placed the crystal ball on a shelf, and immediately strange things began to happen. Every time someone walked by it, a whoosh of icy air swept over them. Objects in the shop moved in the night. A medium who was visiting peered into the crystal ball and saw the spirit of Madame Nora trapped inside. She explained that Madame Nora used to work as a fortune-teller in the market's early days. When she described Madame Nora, the shop owner gasped. She sounded exactly like the old woman who'd dropped off the crystal ball!

> It is said to be the most haunted place in the northwestern United States.

Our next ghost haunted a toy store. He was a mischievous four-year-old boy who liked to move toys around and knock them over. He also thought it was funny to change the time on the clocks. Despite this, the store's manager wanted Jacob—that's the name she gave the ghost—to feel welcome, so she made up a bed for him in the back room and piled it with stuffed animals. Children often left behind toys or notes for Jacob. Some mornings, their gifts would be discovered in a different part of the store, as if Jacob had spent the night playing with them!

Then there are the ghostly stable boys. When the market opened in 1907, farmers brought their produce in by horse-pulled wagon. The animals were cared for by young boys, many who lived in a nearby orphanage. The ghosts, who now hang out by an old wooden ramp, are thought to be those long-ago boys. We're out of room but not out of ghosts, so we'll leave it to you to hunt down the rest!

WEST VIRGINIA
THE MOTHMAN MYSTERY

If you live in West Virginia, you've likely heard the creepy urban legend of the Mothman. The story supposedly starts in November 1966, in a cemetery along the Elk River near Clendenin. Five men were digging a grave. One man paused, glanced up, and was startled to see a large human-like figure with wings in place of arms. He gasped in terror. It flew out from the surrounding woods, gliding silently over their heads then disappearing from sight. What was *that*? None of the men could come up with a logical explanation.

Several days later, two young couples—Roger and Linda Scarberry and Steve and Mary Mallette—were driving in a car together through what is now the McClintic Wildlife Management Area near Point Pleasant. Suddenly, in front of them stood a six or seven-foot tall man-like creature with wings. Its muscular body was covered in dark grayish fur. In the car's headlights, its menacing eyes glowed red.

Roger was behind the wheel and now he sped in the direction of town. But the Mothman followed! With wings that spanned ten feet, it glided effortlessly above their car. Roger floored the gas. The speedometer passed seventy miles per hour. Then eighty. The Mothman kept pace, even when the car reached one hundred miles per hour! They reached Point Pleasant and screeched into the police station. But when they looked up and around, the Mothman had vanished.

> In the car's headlights, its menacing eyes glowed red.

The next day, the headline of the local newspaper read: "Couples See Man-Sized Bird . . . Creature . . . Something!" The story spread like wildfire. Over the next few weeks, the police received almost one hundred additional accounts from residents. Upon seeing the creature, many claimed to have felt a deep sense of dread. Some locals wondered if the Mothman was living in the nearby vacant nuclear power plant, but police found no evidence of the creature or anyone there.

Then, in December 1967, the Silver Bridge which spanned the icy Ohio River in Point Pleasant, collapsed. Forty-six motorists lost their lives. Some witnesses claimed they had seen the Mothman standing on the bridge the day before. They speculated that the creature had been an omen, arriving to warn the town about the deadly disaster. And immediately after the collapse, Mothman sightings stopped altogether.

WISCONSIN
HOMERUN OF HAUNTINGS

The team bus rumbled to a stop in front of the big, fancy Pfister Hotel, and the athletes stepped off. Tomorrow was their game against the Milwaukee Brewers. As they filed into the lobby, one player looked around and let out a gasp of fear. He remembered the last time the team had stayed in this hotel—and the ghosts that had kept him up all night.

He's not alone. Many Major League Baseball players have had supernatural encounters at the Pfister Hotel. Outfielder Carlos Gómez stayed here in 2008, while playing for the Minnesota Twins. He was in the shower when he heard voices in his room. Wrapping himself in a towel, he went to investigate. No one was there. Suddenly his MP3 player, which he'd left on a table across the room, switched on! Static blared out. The device began to shake and move toward the edge of the table all on its own. Gómez lunged, as if diving for a fly ball, and caught it before it fell. He turned it off then placed it back on the table. As he walked away, the device mysteriously flicked on again. He ran for the lobby, holding his pants and shoes!

Pitcher C. J. Wilson said his lamp began to flash wildly on and off when he stayed here while playing for the Texas Rangers. His teammate, infielder Michael Young, claimed he heard phantom footsteps. When he was with the Los Angeles Angels, first baseman Ji-Man Choi reported a misty spirit hovering over his bed as he was trying to fall asleep. Some players have gotten so freaked out they've requested to share a room with another teammate. Los Angeles Dodgers shortstop Mookie Betts, who said he isn't afraid of ghosts, found another place to stay when his team checked in.

Many MLB players have had supernatural encounters at the Pfister Hotel.

But one baseball team has never been bothered by ghosts at the historic hotel: the home team! Brewers players report having peaceful, quiet nights. Some wonder if the mischievous ghost is Charles Pfister himself, who founded the hotel with his father in 1893. Back in the early days of baseball, fans would sometimes rap on the windows and knock on the opposing players' doors throughout the night, so they'd show up to the game exhausted and sluggish. Could it be that Charles' spirit is not a good sport?

WYOMING
THE GHOST SHIP

In the early morning hours, dense fog pushed its way across the Wyoming plains. It settled heavily above a stretch of the North Platte River between the towns of Torrington and Alcova at the base of the Snowy Range Mountains. The fog lingered well into the afternoon, and the air grew chillier. All day, a fisherman in waders had stood in the river's shallows, casting out his line. He dropped his rod and stared in disbelief as the fog began to swirl strangely. Picking up speed, it formed an enormous ball of thick mist. Then, like a curtain on opening night, it started to rise, revealing a ghostly ship.

Despite the lack of wind, the old-fashioned wooden ship floated downstream toward the fisherman. Long icicles hung from its towering masts. Its large sails were encrusted with a shimmery blue-white frost. Upon its deck, a crew of haggard sailors in threadbare, frost-covered clothes huddled in a semi-circle. They stared down at a corpse draped in a canvas sheet. As one of them began to pull back the edge, the fisherman howled. He turned, forcing himself to look away. The ghost ship was an omen of death!

The spectral sailing ship may appear on the river during afternoons of thick fog.

This spine-tingling ship was supposedly first spotted on the North Platte River in 1862 by a trapper. The story goes that when the canvas was pulled back, he saw his fiancée. Then the ship vanished. A month later, he returned home from the wilderness, but his beloved was not waiting for him. He learned she had died—on the exact date he had seen her apparition! About twenty years later, a cattle rancher was the next to encounter the ship of spirits. He saw his wife's body on the deck. He rushed home and breathed a sigh of relief when he found her alive. But later that day, she dropped dead for no apparent reason. About twenty years after that, a farmer splitting wood by the riverbank spied the ship. This time, the corpse on board was his close friend, and the friend passed away that same day.

According to lore, the spectral sailing ship may appear on the river during afternoons of thick fog. Once the one fated to perish is revealed, the boat vanishes. So if the ghostly galley ever shows up, close your eyes tight and run far, far away!

WASHINGTON, D.C.
THE MOST FEARSOME FELINE

Legend has it there's a phantom cat that stalks the basement of the U.S. Capitol building and prowls the halls of the White House. It's been seen so often that it has its own nickname: Demon Cat, or D.C. for short. D.C. is also the abbreviation for the District of Columbia, home of our nation's capital and the buildings this cat haunts.

Demon Cat is not just any old fearsome feline. It has two supernatural missions. Mission #1: frighten anyone who sees it. Whenever a guard or police officer encountered D.C. on their nightly rounds, it was the size of a tabby cat. Aw, what a cute little kitty! they thought. Then, right before their terrified eyes, the cat would grow larger and larger until it was the size of a tiger! Some said it expanded to the size of an elephant. The enormous cat would bare its teeth and prepare to pounce. Then . . . *poof!* It disappeared, serving up a full-on fright.

Before their terrified eyes, the cat would grow larger and larger.

In many cultures, cats are seen as mystical creatures that can foretell bad omens—and D.C. is no different. Mission #2: warn of an impending disaster or tragedy. Night guards in the White House claimed to have spotted D.C. lurking about immediately before the 1865 assassination of President Abraham Lincoln, the October 1929 stock market crash that caused the Great Depression, and the 1963 assassination of President John F. Kennedy!

The feline's first recorded appearances were during the Civil War, when the basement of the U.S. Capitol was turned into a bakery to feed Union soldiers. Soon, the Capitol was overrun with rats attracted by the giant sacks of wheat stored there. How do you get rid of a lot of hungry rats? With a lot of hungry cats! Many suspect that D.C. was one of them. The cats' offspring continued to roam freely throughout the building for generations. Feline pawprints pressed into the cement floor of the Small Senate Rotunda probably came from one of them. Also carved into the same cement floor are the mysterious initials D.C. Is it the mark of Demon Cat?

A GHOST HUNTER'S GUIDE

Did you hear a spooky noise in your attic? Or smell a strange odor coming from the school gym? Or witness a book floating off the library shelf? If so and you want to know more, you may want to gather your friends and go on a ghost hunt! Ghost hunters are like detectives for the supernatural. They search for evidence to prove that a ghost is haunting a particular location. Ghost hunting can be very spooky—and a lot of fun. Before you set out, you'll need to prepare and gather supplies.

Step 1: Prepare

Do research

First visit your local or school library to learn about a location's haunted history. Read about who lived there and what happened. You'll be able to communicate better with a ghost if you know their story.

Ask permission

You must ask and receive permission to investigate a private property. If you don't, it's called trespassing, which is against the law. And if you see a posted sign that says Do Not Enter, don't go in! The warning is for your safety.

Buddy system—always!

Never go ghost hunting alone. Bring friends or family. Besides being safer, it's more fun in a group. And always let an adult know where you are going.

Step 2: Gather Your Ghost Hunter Gear

Flashlight
To help you see in the darkness. Don't forget extra batteries.

Notebook and pen
To write down anything you find interesting or think may be important later. Log not only what you see but also what you feel, smell, and hear. Make a list of the haunted locations you'd like to visit and questions to ask a ghost. You can also draw pictures and maps.

Magnifying glass
To examine ghostly evidence or to read tiny print on gravestones.

Weather thermometer
To measure changes in temperature at a haunted location, which could show a spirit is present.

Compass
To help locate a haunting. If the needle twitches or has a problem finding magnetic north, it could mean there's otherworldly energy.

Voice recorder
To record what's known as electronic voice phenomena (EVP), or sounds a ghost makes.

Camera
To snap an image of the apparition or the spooky spot.

Smartphone
To have several ghost hunting tools in one spot—camera, voice recorder, flashlight, compass. You also never know when you'll need to call someone.

Jacket or sweatshirt
To keep warm. Ghost hunting can give you the chills!

Water bottle and snacks
To keep you hydrated and happy. A hungry ghost hunter is a cranky ghost hunter—and no one wants that! Be sure to pack nutritious, quiet snacks—going CRUNCH! can spook the spirits.

SPOOKY GLOSSARY

There are many ways to say "ghost."
Some common synonyms are phantom, specter, and spirit.

Apparition

a transparent, ghostly figure

Cemetery

a place for burying the dead

Corpse

a dead body

Crypt

compartment inside a mausoleum
that holds the casket or coffin

Cryptid

creature found in folklore whose
existence is unproven

Curse

a calling for harm or injury to come
to someone

Epitaph

an inscription on a gravestone in
memory of the person buried there

Ghost

a spirit of the dead

Gravestone

a stone that marks a grave, also
tombstone

Materialize

appear in physical form

Mausoleum

an above-ground building that
stores bodies of the dead. They are
sometimes built in areas with a lot of
flooding or used by families.

Medium

someone who claims a special ability
to communicate with the dead

Omen

something that is taken as a sign of
what will happen in the future

Orb
a transparent ball of light energy connected to spirits

Ouija board
a game board decorated with letters and numbers that some people believe can be used to communicate with the dead

Petrified
so frightened that one cannot move

Pipe organ
musical instrument often found in churches and concert halls. It produces sound when air is pushed through differently pitched pipes.

Poltergeist
a ghost that moves objects or furniture around or makes unexplained noises. Poltergeists are annoying but not harmful.

Séance
a meeting to summon the dead

Urban legend
a story about a spooky event passed from one person to another that many believe to be true but probably is not

Vampire
a former human who drinks blood and is immortal (can live forever)

Witch
a person believed to have magical powers

111

For Dan, my partner in life and beyond.—S.K.

Haunted USA © 2025 Quarto Publishing plc.
Text © 2025 Heather Alexander L.L.C.
Illustrations © 2025 Sam Kalda.

First published in 2025 by Wide Eyed Editions,
an imprint of The Quarto Group.
100 Cummings Center, Suite 265D, Beverly, MA 01915, USA.
T (978) 282-9590 www.Quarto.com

The right of Sam Kalda to be identified as the illustrator and Heather Alexander to be identified as the author of this work has been asserted by them in accordance with the Copyright, Designs and Patents Act, 1988 (United Kingdom).

All rights reserved.

No part of this publication may be reproduced, stored in a retrieval system, or transmitted, in any form, or by any means, electrical, mechanical, photocopying, recording, or otherwise without the prior written permission of the publisher or a license permitting restricted copying.

ISBN 978-0-7112-9736-4

The illustrations were created in graphite pencil
Set in TXC Pearl, Birch Standard, Acumin Variable Concept
Designer: Sasha Moxon
Commissioning Editor: Alex Hithersay
Production Controller: Robin Boothroyd
Art Director: Karissa Santos
Publisher: Debbie Foy

Manufactured in Guangdong, China TT042025

9 8 7 6 5 4 3 2 1

The author and publisher make no claims regarding the truth of these stories, which are based on local legends, folklore, and personal accounts of purported supernatural activity. This book is not intended to harm or damage the reputation of any individual, business, or establishment. All entries are presented as they have been historically represented or reported.